Wild Woman
—— Memoir in Pieces ——

Cindy Cunningham

Unzipped ——  —— *Issue I*

Wild Woman
Memoir in Pieces

First published in 2020 by
Life in 10 Minutes Press
Richmond, VA

lifein10minutes.com/press

Distributed by IngramSpark
& Life in 10 Minutes Press

ISBN 978–1–949246–06–3

Printed in the United States of America

First Printing, 2020

About *Life in 10 Minutes*

Life in 10 Minutes is a community of writers sharing stories that are brave and true through classes, workshops, retreats, zoom, and our online lit mag. Visit **lifein10minutes.com** to read deep, strange, hilarious, heartbreaking, and powerful stories written 10 minutes at a time, and share yours, too!

Homegrown in Richmond, Virginia, *Life in 10 Minutes Press* began with the mission to give passage to books we believe in. We seek to bring readers titles that are brave, beautiful, raw, heartfelt, and vital, and to nurture authors in their publishing journeys. Learn more at **lifein10minutes.com/press**.

Our mission: We are especially passionate about memoir by women and under-represented voices, nonfiction that challenges the status quo, and boundary-breaking books of all genres. All works published with Life in 10 Minutes Press *are carefully chosen to support our mission and reflect our commitment to promoting fresh, engaging, high-quality storytelling.*

Welcome to *Unzipped*

Life in 10 Minutes fosters love of the immediate. Of the present. The truth. As close up as we can possibly get. At *Life in 10 Minutes*, we reveal life in this moment, right here, right now. Feelings and memories rise from our bodies and spill onto the page. Our stories have curled into knots in our stomachs, fists squeezed around our hearts, pressure against our lungs. We allow these stories to unfurl in our notebooks, releasing us from their grip. As we write, we heal ourselves. As we share our stories, we heal each other. As we heal each other, we heal the world.

Never before has healing the world felt more urgent than right now. Now, when connection is more tenuous and precious than ever. When truth is on the chopping block. When the world is on literal and metaphorical fire, when unhealed family and systemic and global trauma threatens to pull us into our most base and destructive selves.

Writing and sharing and reading our stories allows us to process the past, ground in the present and move into the future, freer and more deeply woven into the life-giving, rich fabric of human life.

When we write unzipped, we reveal the naked truth, the maskless selves, the vulnerable core. When we write unzipped, we join a community of other writers who agree to hold each other's stories and bear witness, to listen, to believe. To create space for the sacred and profane to exist together on the page.

Punctuation is not our first priority. You might find minor errors or typos. You might see a mistake on the page. Sometimes the writing will reflect the chaotic messiness of urgency. We decided that getting the work out there was more important than getting everything perfect.

This quarterly will share the work of writers who have allowed their truth, their trauma, their pain and struggle, their infinite beauty and whispers of hope to breathe life on the page. We are so excited to share them with you.

With love,
Cindy Cunningham and Valley Haggard, Co-Editors
Llewellyn Hensley, Creative Director
Nadia Bukach, Director of Operations

Contents

I Maiden

continued

II Whore

III Crone

About Cindy Cunningham

Cindy Cunningham holds a BA in Psychology from Wake Forest University, an MFA in creative writing from Virginia Commonwealth University, and a PhD in Literature from Georgia State University. She teaches at the Appomattox Regional Governor's School for Arts and Technology (ARGS) in Petersburg, VA where she has served as Chair of Literary Arts since 2002. In addition, she's an instructor at *Life in 10 Minutes* in Richmond, VA. Cindy writes memoir, essays, and poetry, and sits on the Board of the nonprofit, Richmond Young Writers. She is currently at work on both a full-length memoir and a poetry manuscript.

Bittersweet Swallows, her poetry Chapbook was published by Finishing Line Press in 2013. Her poem, "Good Luck Charm," was selected to appear in *Aethlon: XXXVI:2 Spring 2019 / Summer 2019 THE JOURNAL OF SPORT LITERATURE Special Issue: Teaching Sport Literature.*

Her greatest teaching accomplishments are earning the title "Empress of Safe Spaces," from an L10 group and "Most Real Teacher" from a high school group. There's no honor higher.

Acknowledgements

I would like to thank the following folks:

My Tuesday Night Writing Class who wrote alongside me when I was a student and my Tuesday Night Writing Class when I transitioned to instructor. Special thanks to the particularly dedicated members who stick with me again and again: Carrie Sue Casey, Elizabeth Eley, and Amanda S. Thanks, also, to the newest members who dubbed me *Empress of Safe Places.*

Thanks to the readers of various drafts — from 90,000 word versions to this 20,000+ version: Elizabeth Ferris for tackling the first, unwieldy and wild mess of a manuscript and making some sense of it; Gail Giewont who has read my words in so many versions that I can't even recall how many. Her insightful questions and engaged comments sparked me to revise my syntax, my memories, and my life — all for the better. Thanks for never giving up on me. Suzanne Laventure — thank you, sister, for always responding with honesty and from a place of love. One day maybe we can laugh about it all.

For James Stoneking who makes the coffee, fixes the internet connection, and the printer, and the dpi of the photo scan, who reads the drafts, and never complains, at least out loud.

For my permanent and persistent cheerleaders—Bird Cox, Melissa Face, Julie Geen, Sarah Luong, Kimberly Marye, Rosie Messer, Patty Smith. I could do none of this without you.

Llewellyn Hensley for creating the sexy and sassy *Unzipped* logo, the perfect layout, and my stunning cover art. Your creativity, talent, and patience with our ever-changing suggestions knows no measure. I might have given up without your timely, unconditional encouragements along the way. Thank you!

Nadia Bukach for seamlessly operating and organizing meetings, advertising, and calendar details, for creating my fantastic website, for being on the cheerleading team, and for writing stunning work of her own.

For my ARGS students who helped me discover a meaningful career, a reason for waking up.

For all the wild women who helped me survive.

Also, for the few wild men to whom I also owe a debt of gratitude.

Valley Haggard, for showing up and showing up and showing up. For sending notes and drawings and cards and small gifts just when I am on the verge of giving up. For inviting me on writing retreats and conferences and into the L10 community. For never doubting in my ability to achieve ANYTHING I want. For loving me unconditionally. For listening and adapting. For being my long-lost twin at times, my surrogate mother at other times, my wild woman counterpart (until the clock strikes 9 p.m. and we both turn into pumpkins.) For demanding my stories.

Introduction

These fragments I have shored against my ruins.
— T.S. Eliot, *The Wasteland*

Wild Woman—Memoir-in-Pieces originated in ten-minute, furiously scribbled increments in Valley Haggard's Tuesday Night *Life in 10 Minutes* classes held in a small room above Chop Suey Books. Filled with pain and stories and without ever having written nonfiction, I tentatively clicked the registration button online. Signing on for the class seemed like a whim but fate played its role because from the first moment Valley welcomed me to her Halfway House for Writers, I knew I had found my way home.

For several years I filled notebooks with ten minute, unzipped confessions, word play, pain, humor, inadvertent lies that morphed into truths under the microscope of revelation. Then, after much encouragement (gentle arm twisting) I gathered these notebooks and transformed them into a 90,000 word manuscript (monstrosity) that attempted to cover every aspect of my life. Grappling with this material for a few additional years taught me more about myself than did decades of counseling. I both advise against and advocate for the process of wrestling with the angel of your memoir—it all depends on your ability to withstand psychological torture. You also have to accept that the first (100) drafts are going to be terrible.

When Valley and I decided to create *Unzipped*, I knew it was time to explode my unwieldy manuscript, to kill my darlings, to rescue only the vibrant moments.

What you are about to read is a novella-sized version of my memoir revealed through a series of vignettes, shards that form a mosaic of my life.

Welcome to my memoir in pieces.

I
Maiden

I am

I am from a mess of grits, from fatback and fried bologna. I am from warm potato salad, Crisco fried chicken, and lard biscuits.

I am from bare feet from May 1st to Labor Day, porch-sitting stories, sticky hot summers cooled by lemonade, and June bugs rising in droves. I am from *Curious George* and fairy tales, from Mr. Roger's *Neighborhood of Make Believe* where I discovered the name for my first kitten — *ornithorhynchus anatinus* — the baby platypus. We called the kitten *kitty.*

I'm from a revolving door of cats, white cats for years, then golden ones, then gray, then black, then white again. My dad secretly buried any he found dead. I thought cats lived forever.

I am from a world of trick-or-treaters who scared no one except my parents. My mother warned my sister and me of many false dangers, but rarely of any tangible ones. I am not from razor blades in apples, only from the fear of them, but I did experience terror at the words and hands of church officials, boys in parks, and men in public spaces.

I am from a world so alien to me now that sometimes I think I am lying when I imagine growing up in that world. Did I make up the absurdity of my father, the dull beating heart of my mother after work, the bullet-forging neighbors? No positive parental role models emerged from my childhood. No childhood parents who shared kind words; no "there, there" with a hand on my shoulder; no tools with which to build a life.

Vampire

A vampire inhabits my basement, lurks beneath the steps, causes my first blatant lie. My mother clomps down the stairs, demands to know why everything reeks of Lysol. The cool cylinder behind my back shines as a beacon of my sin; my mother's face blotches red, her exasperation evident, but I cannot confess that I needed to spray the evil from the home, to hide the smell of body, to protect us from the creature under the stairs. He'll kill me if I tell.

The vampire had swooped on me in the closed-off basement room as my grandmother sat on the basement stairs humming; I stayed very quiet so she wouldn't be afraid. Brown shag carpet burned hickeys into my shoulder blades, yellow drips of dried paint on the concrete walls like slugs marking imaginary trails as the black-cloaked figure tried to suffocate me. As he bent toward my throat, cape fluttering about me, I floated above my body. As an adult, this trick returns unbidden at the dentist, or during painful medical procedures, or when my emotions surface; lightheaded, I rise to the ceiling, only my toes wiggling, grounding me to my earthly form. In retrospect, the vampire seems an obvious reification of abuse, but because my child mind linked the act to a vampire, I'm never able to excavate the details, the who, what, or why, but the where sticks with me—the basement of wickedness, the dungeon of lies.

I learn to turn my mind to story.

First Grade Semiotics

I am in the first grade, my first year of school. Breathing in crisp pages of *Dick and Jane*, my head spins a bit at these stark red and yellow figures, bicycles and balls, and letters that activate stories in my mind, simple illustrations and letters that manifest meaning. I complete the homework packet for the month in one evening, read all of the first grade books in one month. The teachers let me pass under the arch that links the first and second grade classrooms, and I complete two years in one. I thirst for knowledge.

In the outdoor landscape, the world becomes my text. I seek symbols and skills and power—despise stupid dresses that snag on trees; I learn donkey flips, tree climbing, crabapple bombing in the daylight. Anthropomorphizing all, I speak to trees, attempt to heal their wounds with olive oil and massages and improvised stone magic. For a time I beg pardon to the grass for walking on it: *Please forgive me. I don't know another way to go.*

Indoors, I apologize to each piece of silverware as I close it into the dreary, coffin-like drawer. *Dear spoon, I promise to wake you for breakfast, please don't fight with fork tonight. I hope you understand.*

I don't want to close the drawer. I dance between a life of wild abandon and a desperate drive to find forgiveness for being alive.

Vast differences surface between me and my family—our clothing preferences (mine is haphazard and whatever goes on the fastest; theirs involves something called "matching" and "appropriateness,") hairstyles (mine is pure "ragamuffin" while theirs involves mirror time, "teasing," hairspray, and styling tools), belief (mine is wide open and loving of others but damning of myself; theirs is the reverse.) *Maybe,* I think, *I am an actual alien.*

No common ground exists within family, but the world beyond offers much—roll-a-bat, tag, crabapple wars, beehives, fireflies, and butter-flies, but, later I also find treehouses and cigarettes, bullets forged in a basement next door, and secret games of mommy and daddy and doctor.

Vastation

I've got the peace that passes understanding
Down in my heart, (where?!)
Down in my heart, (where?!)
Down in my heart,
I've got the peace that passes understanding
Down in my heart, (where?!)
Down in my heart to stay.

We have come from revival. Campfire sing-a-longs, Trinity Tag, and Bible-verse baseball. I've won the Best Little Camper award, received a large, cardboard blue ribbon about half the size of my body. In the final group prayer among the adults and the other 7-year-olds, the holy spirit arrived—something mysterious, something that caused my throat to tighten, my eyes to burn, but also hushed me. I don't share this with my sister or my parents; this feels like a secret.

God, do you hear me? Here in the back of a beat-up car, humming the Peace that Passeth Understanding, trying to hold back tears? I think I might see you in the streaked rays of sunlight — the ones that look like the rays of angels, like rays to a promised land? Can those beams carry me to heaven? Can I join you right now so I can sit on the knee of Jesus like in all the pictures at church?

I know I have to get baptized, must step out of my pew next time they sing "Just As I Am." That's my favorite altar call; the preacher always looks me right in the eye. No one likes me JUST as I am — I'm too silly, I eat too much, but I'm just a string bean, I run into things because I can't slow down, but every time I hear that hymn, a ghostly presence fills the sanctuary, touches folks right on their hearts, can stop them or fill them with Jesus. The preacher whispers secrets to the people who kneel with him and the choir and congregation sometimes sing every single verse or repeat the chorus over and over and you can almost feel the rafters humming. The preacher and the sinner just kneel there, *embracing*; they always cry. Maybe sneaking up and listening just once wouldn't be so bad?

In the dark car, huddled in the back seat, I mouth the words to the hymn, *Just as I am, I come, I come!* I strike up courage and ask my mom if I can be baptized, preparing my way to heaven.

***

At the last minute, Mom can't decide whether I should wear the shorter half slip with a white T-shirt or the longer full slip under my long, white baptismal robe even though she bought the full slip special for the occasion. A little lace and a yellow embroidered flower line the top. I want to wear my bathing suit — I'm just going to get all wet anyway, but Mom tells me not to be silly, of course I can't wear a *bathing suit* to my baptism. Plus, I have to wear all white. I forget why. She also can't find her roll of film and is yelling at my dad to help her, calling him Robert instead of Bob, so it's serious; she seems a little crazy. My sister and I scarf down the buttery sugar cake from a local bakery, a treat usually reserved for Christmas mornings.

It's not magical or sacred in the baptistery like I thought it would be — it looks like a big blue baby pool with steps and plastic walls, but the preacher stands waist deep in the water and holds his hand out to me and I take the two steps down. The water feels warm like lake water on a summer's afternoon, and the preacher asks the questions we practiced the day before about believing that Jesus is the son of God and that he rose from the dead and that I will take him to be my personal lord and savior. I say I do believe and cross my arms like I'm doing the dead man's float. As he baptizes me "in the name of the Father, the Son, and the Holy Spirit," the preacher puts one arm around my shoulders and lays one hand on my crossed arms and forgets to remind me to hold my breath.

When I rise, coughing, water up my nose and down my throat, he puts a white towel to my face and somewhat forcefully guides me to the stairs leading out. I worry that maybe something went wrong; this was supposed to be the biggest moment of my life and every sin would be washed away and my new life would begin, but I just feel embarrassed and wet and cold. Actual snot may have come out of my nose.

My mother is very proud of me as she takes me to dry my hair and change my clothes. She even pats me on the back with the towel.

Years later she will tell me I must have been baptized too early — that it didn't stick.

**

About a month after my baptism, a thunderstorm drenches me in the front yard. Arms raised, I beg for a lightning bolt to take this new purified me to heaven — why won't God take me NOW that I am born again? Science class taught me that moving closer to trees will attract lightning, so I stand very close, my feet pressed hard to the ground, rain water washing me clean.

Then a vision or a vastation — another me, a me at age 35 stands in a shower and extends a hand to the seven-year-old me and says, "You will make it here." This feels simultaneously horrendous — 35 years is even longer than Jesus stayed on earth — and maybe a little comforting — maybe I will survive childhood after all; maybe it gets better.

Learning the Boundaries

The first time I ran away, I was two. My mom entrusted me to my dad for the first time ever, and when she returned from her appointment, she could not find me anywhere. My father let me play in the yard but told me to stay within the boundary. We lived on an Air Force Base, so the MPs and friends began a search. Apparently the "big kids" marching around the base imitating Airmen proved irresistible — wearing my sparkling red Dorothy Gale shoes, Mardi Gras type beads, a large bow taped to my Mohawk to indicate my gender, and a diaper, I jumped right in line. The big kids said they didn't notice me until too late.

The subsequent flights seemed more intentional.

***

I am in the 9th grade, a year younger than the others, fascinated by the bright pink lipstick and pitch-black hair of my English teacher who is off on another tangent about her love for Robert Redford;

maybe she's at least tying it to *Gatsby* this time. A light tapping at the small classroom window reveals Patti Dorr's worried, freckled face, her hair sparking in static electricity. She lives at least twenty miles from this school. This is before the days of cellphones, and she doesn't have my class schedule. How does no one notice this bright-red-haired gal peering into various classrooms looking for me? It seems like all the adults went blind in the 1980s.

She feels like dying on a fairly regular basis and when she says she needs me, I always go with her without question. Since my 7th birthday, I have understood that the darkness of suicide can descend without an external trigger; also, understanding triggers does not always solve the problem anyway. Patti never shares details of her life beyond me and our experiences. On this day, as I slip out of the classroom door with my bathroom pass, she slides up the sleeve of her jacket to reveal the map of fiery red and cross-stitched scars on her forearms, looks me dead in the eye and says, "You are the only one who cares. You are the only one who can save me."

I'm not sure why "you are the only one who can [fill in blank]" slays me. Throughout the years, "But you're the only one" could make me drop my drawers, run away from home, steal bologna from a convenience store, quit my job, empty my bank account. A sucker for being the only one who could bring happiness or safety to someone: I admit, at times I crave this still. Of course fallacy rifles this concept — no person can complete another, but on that day, I believe, and we saunter right out the school's front door, directly past the main office; no one questions us, no one stops us. Invisible, invincible?

Patti talks a mile a minute; she wants to head 250 miles north to Colonial Heights, VA, where her dealer friend can put us up for a few days while she gets her head on straight. She's holding my hand and making grand gestures, sometimes walking backward, sometimes hopping on the pavement, or balancing on the curb like it's a tight-rope. I take even and steady steps. At some point, I learned that only civilians bounce when they walk. Good soldiers do not bounce. I don't know why I want to be a good soldier; I'm a pacifist.

After walking a few miles, we hitch a ride to Wake Forest University from a waitress who tries to talk us out of hitchhiking. She wears a skin tight black and white outfit, fishnet stockings (that I did not know to call fishnets at the time), an apron, and a frilly collar. Years later, I notice that they wear similar outfits at the *Silver Fox,* an exotic dance club. She warns us about the dangers of getting rides from strangers, that men will take advantage of us, that we could end up on the news, or in a trunk, or in a ditch by the side of the road, but the admonitions seem absurd to us; we are invincible; we are thirteen; nobody will mess with *us.*

Patti refuses to think about money or food or changes of clothes; the mundanity of details and preparation would ruin any adventure: "We'll get by on looks, promise. You can get anything if you know what to say. I'll show you, promise. I just need a cigarette, man, I am *dying* over here." I know she really means we'll get by on *her* looks as she flips her hair, hand on her hip, cocked like a mini movie star. She stands just under 5 foot, but her energy is palpable. If she dazzles me, of course she'll dazzle everyone. I feel no undercurrent of warn-ing; I follow her, starstruck.

When we reach Wake Forest, and the waitress-dancer pulls away, Patti sticks her thumb out once more. A young minister pulls over after only a few minutes and even though he freaks me out a little, my friend turns on her daughter-of-a-preacher charm and convinces him that we are college students—tiny, tiny college students—and talks him into buying us two bus tickets to Virginia by telling him that her mother or sister or someone important has died; she swears to pay him back, gets his contact information, kneels with him in prayer, and even I believe her for a moment, lost in the power of story. The minister drives us to the bus station, purchases two tickets, then waves us on, perhaps feeling like he has accomplished a good deed, only one small flash of hesitation crossing his face—at the time I imagine he worries about getting that money back, but in retrospect, I believe he must have felt a premonition, or guilt.

The only time I have ridden a bus, other than a school bus, is when our 5th grade class visited Washington D.C. This is not that crowd. In the front sit older women and men, some who nod off, mouths open, drooling; others clutch bags between their knees, furtive; the middle rows blend with younger men and women who seem to be what my mother would call *down on their luck,* and I cannot quite make out the people in the back through the cigarette smoke. The driver recommends that we sit toward the front, but Patti guides me about halfway back, then, once we hit the road, she whispers, "Be right back," slips me a sly grin and sends me a trucker. He might be the biggest man I have ever met, lumberjack-size. The kind whose muscles threaten to break through flannel when he leans forward, the kind whose veins pop on his forearms when he flexes. His hair curls blond like my current junior high crush who has not even had a genuine growth spurt.

The trucker introduces himself as Sam, passes me a pint of whiskey. As he leans forward, Aqua Velva also leans forward, the scent of my father, of protection, and Sam says, "Your friend says you'd like some company," and I cannot refuse. I am southern; I am a girl; I am on the run; I am a soldier who follows orders and doesn't want to stand out. I fake a swig, but my lips burn anyway and then his mouth covers mine and I succumb to the softness of flannel, the hardened trucker's body, the scent of cologne and cigarettes on a Greyhound bus. He smells like daddy. He is 28; he praises my maturity as his fingers crack open my body.

The rest of the journey fades, but Sam asks for my phone number when we're disembarking; I probably give it to him. I am very polite. Patti said she'd teach me how to survive, but I didn't catch on that survival meant stuffing it all inside, letting men take what they want.

We are thirteen. We are invincible. We are invisible.

It's freezing, but we arrive in Virginia too late to call anyone, so we creep into the Petersburg Laundromat, warm up the monster dryers with the few quarters we can scrounge up, and then climb inside, fetal. Smushed against each other, her whiskey cigarette breath warms my face; the slight smell of sex on her fingers comforts me in a way that confuses me.

"I hope nobody sticks a quarter in the slot — we'll be dead meat."

Giggles of girls in dryers, in tight jeans and flowy tops, in the middle of an adventure.

"So, how was SAM?" More laughter.

My vagina hurts, but I don't mention that. I also don't ask why she left me alone.

No one ever believes that we fit into those machines, but we curl right into the black and white speckled spinners until some adults arrive and when they are not looking, we bolt to the back of the building, darting from blower to blower, catching the random heat in the winter freeze. When the blowers stop, we race through the streets belting out "Free Bird" and playing mad air guitar for the extended riff, whooping and congratulating ourselves for getting it right. I bounce and leap; I even kiss her once right on the lips. Hugging and twirling until dizzy, we collapse on our backs singing freedom, singing love; we want this forever.

Eventually we need a place to crash, so Patti calls her old buddy, a drug dealer, who meets us at a local convenience store; a woman sits silent, back straight and tense beside him in his car. She doesn't survive that night. In one memory, I see Vincent shoot her right in the head; her silence and lack of pleading stunning. He accuses her of cheating, or stealing drugs, of lying. I could describe this in great detail, but in another, just as valid memory, I only know these details via hearsay. Either way, I never follow up on this. I never research or emote or process. This act seems too alien to appear in any newsprint or factual source. How could this be the life I was living?

Vincent drops us off at Robby's house in Colonial Heights, dark, blackout curtains on the windows, hardwood floors and a musty green couch. Ashtrays overflow, dishes pile in the sink, moldy and rank. Sliding right into the center of the sofa, in between Robby and his roommate who never reveals his name, Patti, oh so wise, proffers herself. Robby pulls out a shoe box of pills. I know most of them — yellow jackets, black beauties, Quaaludes, reds, even a few Benadryl. Offering this box of treats as if he's passing out candy on Halloween, he seems both predatory and vulnerable. Something about pills calls me like a siren's song to sailors — the colors, the ovals, perfectly round edges, the slippery feel on the tongue, the smallness, the absolute sameness — but even we aren't stupid enough to fall for this one — do not take candied drugs from strangers who have nothing else to offer you. In retrospect, he reminds me of Napoleon Dynamite — tall, lanky, orange hair in awkward curls, clueless and angsty.

Patti disappears with the other fella after a while and invites me for a threesome, but I just want to go back where the two of us could hold hands and sing again, where we could be free from this darkness. I don't feel at home and I don't want to talk to these men. The couch itches my back and thighs. I need to pee, but their bathroom reeks, covered in mildew and urine stains. Maybe a television plays; maybe a radio. Maybe I pace the room; maybe I freeze. At some point, Robby demands that someone fuck him or he'll call the cops and turn us in for being runaways, but desperation in others turns us off—we only want to exchange with the powerful, so we refuse. At least I think we do; my memory of that trip twists and turns like a Möbius strip; I remember refusing sex, then giving a blow job; I remember not smoking but lighting butts; I remember heat and a Christmas tree; once I get a handle on a moment, it slides into another.

I do remember the moment I move into being a cutter. Patti goes into the kitchen for a drink of water; I follow her to avoid Robby. She stands with her Frankenstein's-creature-scarred arm over the sink, a steak knife poised over her wrist, no new cuts as yet. Silently, as if playing a role in an old movie, I take the blade and, submitting myself as a sacrifice, slice it across my own wrist. Of course this fails; we both bleed; we both lose; and Robby comes into the kitchen and loses his mind, screaming. "I will not go to jail for two kids killing themselves in my house!" Two kids he tried to seduce with a shoe box of pills; two kids he tried to blackmail into sex. I have a flash of wondering where my all-seeing, all-knowing parents are and why they have not saved me. Why they did not know I had walked out of school, hitched a ride, grabbed a bus, and threw myself into the heart of danger a state away.

The rest of this night blurs into hazy smoke, comings and goings of bikers, dealers, women who rarely spoke. I search my memory, but only flashes arrive—closed blinds, double entendres flying above my head, money changing hands, violence, laughter, a stench, a panic.

The next day, we leave to buy cigarettes, and the cops recognize Patti in the front seat of the truck; she's a familiar face among the Colonial Heights PD. They pull us over, joking about "long time no see," then take us to the station where they call my parents in North Carolina.

They let the driver go, no charges or questions that I remember. I keep flicking at the dried cum on my windbreaker. I can't remember how it got there, but I don't recall taking anything from the shoe box. I also don't recall much from the night before. Patti asks them not to call anyone for her, but they call her sister anyway. Patti rubs her arms, breaking open the scabs. She whispers that if I tell, we'll be separated forever. She confesses that when her minister parents sent her to live with her sister, they told her not to come back unless she straightened up—the next stop would be a return to the psych hospital. I promise to keep any secret she asks of me. I am young enough, still, to believe that love and friendship can cure all pain. We just need more time.

The officers are kind; they offer us vending machine sodas and chips. It seems as though they will try to protect us. I joke around like my daddy does, try to show the police that I am smart and aware and can joke about runaways and cigarettes and boys: the greatest defense mechanism, humor. My parents arrive a few hours later, acting just like parents should. They may have even hugged me—one-armed of course; I am sure my father made many, many jokes. My mother most likely thanked the lord. When we get home, she will stuff me in the shower, then spray me with Lysol from head to toe, telling me that my hormones always get me into trouble.

The four-hour ride home remains mainly a blank. I recall giving my dad the minister's information and saying that Patti and I promised to pay him back; I somehow believe that if I can stamp the event with a religious tone, I will be forgiven. My dad says the preacher should be arrested. I didn't understand what the preacher did wrong. Patti could convince almost anyone of almost anything, so how could we blame the man?

In the core of my 13-year-old heart, I believed in the innate ability of a young girl to tempt an adult man into action.

At times, I still do.

Gourmet

North Carolina, the 1970s, a time when prepackaged foods hit the markets, when mothers leave their homes and enter the workforce whether they want to or not. In the midst of this socio-economic paradigm shift, my mother becomes enamored with the glory of canned, boxed, frozen, and processed foods; she elevates them to *gourmet*. Our family enjoys so many gourmet foods that you wouldn't believe it: Beanie Weenies; Lime Jell-O Fluff Salad, and Hamburger Helper Beef Stroganoff. Any cheese above Kraft slices—yep, gourmet. You can melt blocks of Velveeta on the stove and call it *exotic queso cheese dip*. (To this day I don't think my mother knows that *queso* means cheese.) I grow up on Friday night Totino's frozen pizzas and crispy iceberg salads topped with New Jersey tomatoes, sweet Vidalia onions, and a special homemade Thousand Island dressing made of sweet relish, Miracle Whip, and gourmet Heinz Ketchup. Occasionally we branch out to the all-beef kosher hot dogs, but nothing tastes better than Easy Cheese and Ritz crackers. My sister and I try to capture the art of making a flower out of the spiraling, spaghetti-like processed cheese, but mainly we create blobbed messes. We gobble them up like starving children.

When my sister and I grow older and turn down Velveeta melted cheese and bring over brie to bake instead, my mother declares that college has ruined us with its dangerous liberalism. Proclaiming with great confidence that the "French aren't really known for cheese; they are known for their bread," my mother ignores the baguette, forcefully spreads her port wine cheese ball (*the ALCOHOL is cooked out of course*) onto tiny preheated dinner rolls—you know, the gourmet way.

Psych

When I was 15, I found love in chocolate pie and graham cracker crusts, long telephone conversations on winding corded phones. I discovered Quaaludes and acid. The most popular drug dealer at school dropped 13 hits of acid in his eye and they institutionalized him. When they put me in the psych hospital, I lost my mind.

In the Nuthouse

Here he comes, Dr. J, dragging his baby-duckling interns behind him, all lined up, hoping for a crumb of praise. Yep, there's the pimple-faced, tall intern who never looks me in the eyes but who is more than willing to describe my *affect*. There's the only female intern I have seen — short, wrinkle-browed, always taking notes even though the only thing I EVER say to Dr. J's inane questions is, "I want to go home." What could she possibly write? Today there are five little ducklings.

"How do you feel today?"

"I want to go home."

"How did you sleep last night?"

"I want to go home."

"Well, if you want to go home, we have to make sure you are taking your medications and working through your *issues*." Dr. J's "*w*"s sound like "*v*"s. I imagine him as Dracula even though he is Iranian. His interns scribble away.

"I want to go home."

"Did you have a bowel movement today?"

I never respond to this question. It can earn you an enema.

"Did you enjoy the arts and craft session?"

"I want to go home."

"Is there anything you want to tell me today?"

"I want to go home."

"You know, you cannot keep getting mad at the cat and kicking the dog." His *the* sounds like a *zee* and that's all I can hear. I also do not know who is the cat and who is the dog, but I *would* like to kick him.

The doctor reminds me about group therapy, then signals his duck-lings with a nod and one raised finger. On the way out he speaks of diagnoses and behaviors. He never meets with me one on one. They put me in this place because I chronically run away, but not once has anyone asked me why I run.

They also don't ask about Darlene, who shuffled into my room last week and made me fake-flush my cat-shaped flower down the toilet while she screamed bloody murder.

They never explain my new roommate who woke me up at 3:00 a.m. yelling "HOW OLD ARE YOU?" as she ripped my family photos off the wall. A Daryl-Hannah-from-*Splash* creature — alien, long blonde locks, tall — she emitted a banshee wail, then scratched at my hospi-tal bracelet: "HOW OLD ARE YOU?! HOW OLD ARE YOU?!" The security guards and nurses shot her up with Thorazine and dragged her to solitary. I never saw her again.

No one asks how I feel about the paranoid, rocking, mumbling, Tourette's-like patients. The old women with matted hair, makeup like Bette Davis in *Baby Jane*, caked on in front of tin foil rectangles taped onto cold tile walls. The post-shock therapy patients with blackened eyes and zombie stares. We look like creepy-clown-*Its*, and they treat us like children. We make ceramic ashtrays and belts stamped with mushrooms or balloons. At snack time, we drink juice from tiny, flowered Dixie cups and eat vanilla sandwich cookies. We become first graders again, seeking attention and gold stars for best behavior, but this gets you no closer to leaving the nuthouse; it's just a sham.

We're in the cuckoo's nest, under the bell jar. Don't rock the boat or you'll end up in solitary, or transferred, or in shock therapy, because in the psych ward, your *no* does not matter.

***

Theda and I learn to avoid the common area, to walk the main hall for sanity. She's a 60-something-year-old woman whose husband left her for a man, so she named him devil. To combat this, she became God.

It's midnight, so after the mandatory two hours of attempted sleep, we're finally allowed out of bed; we meet at the payphone by the nurses' station as usual. I grab my Marlboro Reds and she chain smokes Pall Malls; I light them for her, the taste of my cowboy killers blending with her classically mild ones. Her hair is perfectly coiffed as usual, even though her gown is stained with spots of coffee and hints of breakfast. In our shuffles from one end of the hall to the other, she generally does not speak of herself as a deity; we chat about the joys of smoking, her love of horses, the view from the various windows (north overlooks concrete; south overlooks the highway and the mall), how neither of us belongs in this place, how long we think it will be until the lady on the breathing machine will die; she is beginning to sound like Darth Vader.

Today differs.

The nurses agree to let her have a cup of coffee, so we make our way into the nearly empty commons room. Only a few of us are allowed night privileges. We settle in for a chat.

"Do you believe I am God?"

Shit.

I avoided this for weeks. Theda has asked everyone else on the ward. I thought I evaded this by walking and listening and talking with her. She does not always respond well.

"Let's talk about something else. Do you remember your very first horseback ride?"

She leans in close, smoky breath against my face, "Do you believe I am God?"

I cannot lie to her. She is my friend. We avoid the crazy together, right?

"Um...I believe you believe you are God?"

Not enough.

"Do YOU believe I am God?"

Finally, I acquiesce. "I don't believe in *any* God today, but if I did, you'd be it!"

Wrong answer.

Her face morphs into a nearly demonic countenance, one long, bony finger points my way. I jump up from the table. The only word I can understand from her screeching is: "BETRAYER!" Who knew this frail, asthmatic woman could yell so loudly?

Somehow, she manages to climb onto the table, grabs her coffee cup and slings hot, black liquid in my direction. "BETRAYER!" Her hair wild, gown flying, thin, vein-thick arms of sagging flesh like my grandmother's arms peeking through, a frail deity, sere. She begins to preach in earnest, to weep. My heart begins to break.

They take her to solitary.

***

A few weeks after my parents sign me out of the hospital, I overdose. I do not take the 63 amitriptyline from an excess of emotion but because the emotion stops. In that moment, I feel nothing, just a rational acknowledgment that I will continue to disappoint everyone.

There are white lights, thumb-sized tubes up my nose and down my throat, charcoal, I am cursing, I am thrashing, I am threatened with restraints. I am pure, uninhibited fury.

In ICU, my dad jokes, my mom brings homework that I cannot complete, my grandma says people are dying of leukemia and I am selfish so she will not visit. My uncle sends a long letter saying that it gets better. A boy with a crush on me brings me a stuffed kitten. My dad names the kitty "Odie," short for overdose. Blood from my nasal tube permanently stains its left ear and my dad laughs about Odie kitty for years. He finds himself hilarious.

No one asks why I have done this. They do, however, honor my request never to return to Dr. J. In fact, they take me out of therapy altogether.

One of the Cool Kids

When Nadine, a New York transfer student, invites me over instead of spending the night at Mitzi's like I had told my parents, I feel honored. She smokes lots of pot, brags about boys and drugs, and listens to the Ramones and the Sex Pistols instead of Lynyrd Skynyrd, Molly Hatchet, and Nantucket like me and my friends do. Her hair spikes, short in an era of feathered hair, curling irons, and hair spray; she sports a trench coat most days and black boots with silver chains instead of the locals' army jackets and dingo boots. We brandish a redneck chic, but Nadine exudes nihilism.

At her house, a two story in a wealthy neighborhood, she plunks down a bottle of George Dickel and a jug of O.J. She introduces a game where we reveal a secret, then seal it with a shot. Cross-legged on her plush shag carpet, we match shot for shot with O.J. chasers. Her New York City punk glamour diminishes me and I don't remember any of the secrets except for revealing I have not had "real" sex before.

I find out much later that she only shot O.J.

At some point, we [I] stumble to the nearby park where a crowd of ten or so lanky, long-haired South Fork boys hotbox cigarettes and pass around bowls of sickly sweet Sinsemilla. They greet Nadine, as always, like one of the guys; I hang back, knowing them only by reputation. They chug Milwaukee's Best (we call it "The Beast") and smash the empty cans on their heads. Someone's car stereo system pounds out "Sweet Home Alabama"; I take one hit off a bowl. The picnic tables begin to spin; the landscape begins to grey.

I am on my hands and knees on gravel-covered concrete, beside a picnic table underneath a pavilion. I am eye to eye with tattered, wooden benches, and pot leaf belt buckles. I am threatening to throw up on some boy's shoes if he touches me again. Nadine is nowhere to be found. I am surrounded by teenage boys who taunt me, who want to touch me, who want me to do things I do not want to do.

At some point, a young man whose name I do not know leans down, says, "I'll get you out of here," and he ignores the jeers and catcalls and we begin to stumble through the streets, arms locked around each other like soldiers in war, but I am just a drunken mess, and he is just a good, good boy and I think I might be crying in the street and I think HE might be crying in the street; I think I might be calling for Nadine and he might be shushing me; I think he might be standing up to boys who tried to lay a claim to me.

He is not strong; we collapse on the street more than once; he keeps lifting me with all the tenacity of a 14-year-old boy on a moral mission. After what seems like a trek through Mordor, we stumble into his basement where he sets me on the concrete floor, begging me to be quiet, not to puke, and fetches me a blanket and a flannel shirt. My shirt is torn open; I don't remember why or how; I cannot go home like that. He brings me a scratchy dog blanket and a bucket for vomiting, but soon after, his mother comes downstairs because the boy fears I might actually die. She shakes her head, brings me a wet washcloth and a flat pillow, tries unsuccessfully to get my phone number so she can call my parents.

The mom's face blurs as she says I can sleep until the sun rises, but then I must leave. The young man stands watch until dawn, reminds me when I wake that Jimi Hendrix choked on his own puke and died in his sleep.

I always felt lucky that I escaped unscathed, but in retrospect, I no longer consider myself unscathed. I don't remember seeing the fella again. For decades I felt ashamed of this story, ashamed that I lost control and that I didn't know what happened. I experienced no anger, no sadness, only shame. Shame that a young man risked his reputation by being an animal of love, by showing shreds of human kindness. Shame that his mother found me on her floor in a powerless state. Shame that Nadine stopped talking to me. She moved back to NYC a few months later without letting any of us know. I never once questioned the South Fork boys.

I still don't know how it gets so deeply embedded into the psyche never to blame the boys.

II
Whore

Pussy Power

Eventually I decide to embrace the wild one: to perfect the art of sex until I can fuck all night long or have a quickie. My friends and I compare notes on how to get guys off in under five minutes or drag it out until they beg. We leave them begging, weeping, cursing, sleeping. We know power in the back seats of cars, flat patches in the woods, church basements. We slip our hands between our legs, run our fingers under the boy's noses, whisper, "You want some of this?" We're good girls in school, make it through math and science by imagining all the ways we can control the other, pretending that one day the boys might bring us to the same place of ecstasy even though we know we only achieve orgasms when alone, squeaking bed mattresses until fathers on the listen for restlessness appear. We sniff our fingers, prefer the smell of ourselves.

Who wouldn't want a piece of this pussy power?

Prison Detail

Sixteen, just barely licensed to drive, we cruised
I-40 to Greensboro and back, just
for the thrill. We wore Daisy Dukes,
tube tops, bare feet, our
flip flops in the back seat. We took
turns hanging out the window
trying to get a rise out of the prisoners
or the guards, but we never got a rise
out of either, the guards motionless, shotguns
to their shoulders, the prisoners shackled
at the ankles, hands working the earth
or collecting trash, moving in unison
and there we were, driving in circles,
imagining lithe bodies beneath
orange jumpsuits, our youth filled
with catcalls for the unknown,
the impossible, the dangerous.

We thought it our calling to liberate;
the two of us, naive, trapped
in our tortured libidos,
our secret death drives.

The Abuser: Why I Loved Him

He held my hand in public as well as in private.

He cradled me in the crook of his arm.

He let me rub his soft belly like a buddha.

When I walked 15 miles in the snow to see him, he welcomed me with open arms.

He smelled of English Leather, hair products, and cigarettes.

When he discovered that others had my body count among theirs, he flew into a rage. I thought that meant he would protect me.

He listened to, and remembered, every word I said.

Our bodies rhapsodized, body and soul.

Mainly, though, I loved him because he accepted what I proffered, and because he splayed me open like a fish.

Bad Patient

I lie flat with feet in stirrups; I am cold; I have changed my mind. The doctor says it's too late, says I'll just change my mind again. I won't, but my parents and my boyfriend told me this is my option. The doctor makes sure the vacuum tube remains in my line of sight, tells me to keep my eyes open. The nurse lets me put my arm around her waist, lets me hold her hand. The doctor says he hates his job, but never explains why he spends his Saturdays performing abortions at the center.

He tells my father I am a bad patient.

Three days later, with a fever of 106 degrees, I'm taken to the hospital for an emergency D&C (dilation and curettage). The old woman who shares my room overhears my nurse talking about birth control and demands a room change. My father brings in Odie kitty and performs a puppet show from behind the curtain. When I cover my face with the sheet, my mother says, "You know, it was my grandchild too." No one tells my sister where I am. She assumes I have just left home again.

Why I Loved Him: A Redux

It's more than the deep-seated hatred of self, more than tickling my nose on his belly, than PDA, than the softness of his lips and the ways of orgasm. I loved his singing voice and his drummer energy. I loved his scent and a neck where a vampire could get lost and the green of his eyes and the curl of his hair and his love of Judas Priest and I loved that he could tell me that he loved me too. I even loved him when I finally had to break up years too late.

I don't think I stop loving anyone completely.

A few years into the relationship, I stole his green eyes and his curly brown hair and gifted them to my daughter. Took his big belly laugh and passed it down. I didn't mean to transfuse the anger but she inherited that in spades as well as his singing voice and sex drive. When she rages, I fear she will drive a car into a tree or knock me to concrete, but she is not her father and that becomes both easier and harder to remember as we grow older.

Why I Left Him

It was not because he kicked the legs out from under my chair and dropped me on my back in front of the neighbor because I was being "too polite."

Nor was it when he tried to kill the man at the 7-11 who asked me where the *Time* magazines were.

It was not because he slept with Cleo who worked at Burger King or because he got another girl pregnant and then made me talk her through a miscarriage over the phone or because he threw me onto concrete for letting a fish flop back into the water.

It was not for dragging me out of a Judas Priest concert for looking at the drummer, for slapping me when I asked him to slow down when he drove drunk, for belittling, degrading, or being, as my grandmother would say, just plain mean.

I left him when he toasted his sobriety with champagne, then started a fight with a friend, and ended up punching a hole in my parents' bedroom ceiling when they were out. All the while my daughter, two months old, so pure and innocent in her Valentine's Day dress and tights sat propped on pillows, a bright red bow in her hair, hands outstretched waiting to be lifted.

This was why I left him. So many years too late.

There is a Wolf
Also Inside of Me

Many moons later, after completing a year of college and beginning to work a few evenings a week, I venture out a bit. To my great surprise, I turn predatory, no longer the victim. I'm a mama bear at home, wise owl at school, and big bad wolf at night. After work a couple of nights a week, I seek women who turn meek under my passion. I choose younger women with little education, no money, and seduce them with poetry, knowledge from my one whole semester of college, and wine. I'm flipping the script; feeling my feels; envisioning everything on an upswing. Finally I am on the right path.

The day I come home to find my mother sitting on the formal couch with my *Human Sexuality 101* journal and the five-pound family bible open beside each other, everything ceases. Because I am now a lesbian and my parents are fine, upstanding Christians, they take custody of my daughter. The law backs them up.

In the years after, raw pain and grief and anger fill almost every waking moment, and even my dreams turn solely to nightmares. When not attending college or waiting tables or self medicating, I park my car down the road from my parents' house and crawl beneath their living room window. Perched under closed windows, I imagine them singing along to some Disney musical, my mother reading and rocking. Or maybe they are arguing about bedtime routines. I never know whether I want to stumble on their bliss or their pain. Neither will calm the chaos inside of me.

I visit each weekend under direct supervision; being a lesbian means I will mark my child indelibly with sin. My parents allow only certain television shows, backyard play within eyesight, ice cream, or reading certain books. It will take years to earn the privilege of driving her to the park or to my own house. Even though the lawyer told me I have standard custody rights including overnights and weekends, this is a lie. My parents can deny me anything. Not because I ever neglected or harmed my daughter. Not once had anyone ever accused me of being inattentive or a bad mother, not even in the moment.

Not until Nicole was about 5 years old did she see where I lived. For about 10 years I kept a space for her — a child's bedroom, ice cubes made of Kool-Aid, her favorite foods (lots of cheese and dips), a decorated space. These items and spaces confused new friends, and I had to explain too often, so eventually I stopped delineating or dedicating spaces, but they remained in closets and freezers and in sheds.

I could make my house a home at the drop of a hat.

Legalese

I visit my parents' lawyer to discuss the custody agreement. I am a 19-year-old single, lesbian mother in the early 1980s. I enter the leather, glossy office, Mr. Cleland the spitting image of his son I had admired from afar—redheaded, muscled, whose father hosted keg parties for the high school seniors because he deemed it safer to allow the kids to drink under his supervision. He halfway stands, barely sliding his leather puffy chair back, holds out a hand that I do not shake. It takes all I have not to let the southern belle rise and offer my hand, shaking and sweating, to his encompassing grip. He smiles and jokes about the weather or state of affairs of the nation. He pretends our discussion is between equal adults. All we need are martinis and servers in white coats. Hardly anything could bring our discussion to a world less surreal.

Surreal to discuss my daughter's life and wellbeing as if the details can fit on a piece of paper; that no child exists behind that word "custody." No lovely child with Shirley Temple curls, fat cheeks, hands that grip my forearm like a hook, my new reason for living. I am grappled; I am a fish out of water. I am a girl underwater.

I am trusting him as he says I am signing a standard custody agreement with visitation and overnights assumed. We shook on it. I have an IQ of 157, but I am an idiot in the words and ways of law, an imbecile in the words and ways of grown men. My signature gave rights to my parents to decide completely when I could and could not see my daughter.

My daughter and I spend much of our lives suffering from the betrayal of this moment. We both bear abandonment in our bodies—reflux, fibromyalgia, depression.

A motherless child. A childless mother.

Better Off

I needed my own lawyer. Lawyers refused to touch custody cases without more money than I could earn as a waitress and a full-time college student, so I tried to mother as best as I could. I showed up every weekend, showed up even when my parents changed their locks or lied about the times of my daughter's volleyball games or plays or performances. I just kept at it. Stubborn as a bear whose cub remains trapped in a zoo and she cannot fight because she wants the cub to remain safe, but she knows she could protect the cub more effectively than the zoo keepers.

A useless mama bear, I paced a restless futile rage, fearing that any attack would prove me unnatural, uncivilized, a queer, preternatural oops of the cosmos. I did hope, however, that my consistent presence could help guide and protect my daughter.

My confession that I never fought my parents actively causes no end of shame and I want to pretend that even now I let the judgments roll off my back. I have heard them over the years: "Well, I am sure that you and your daughter were both better off," and "But you got a PhD," and "But, look how fucked up you were; how could you raise a kid?" and "You must have done something to deserve this; they wouldn't have just kicked you out for nothing." But I know that we weren't better off, and I know I was a good mother, and I know why they kicked me out, and my PhD meant nothing to me without a daughter who meant everything to me.

I want to weave a happy-ever-after tale where I carry my daughter off into the sunset and we march arm-in-arm against social injustices and say *I Love You* each morning and before bedtime and we trust only the good men and women and we spot the wolves in grandmother's clothing straightaway; but this is not our story. I did not slay a dragon or win a custody battle and the evil stepmother is my real mother who cut out pieces of my heart and fed them back to me and my daughter for decades.

As an adult, my daughter flat out doesn't believe me. I waited so long to speak my truth (into her young adulthood) that she swallows the myth my family weaved—that I abandoned her to pursue higher education. She publicly thanks my mother every Mother's Day for raising her. That, I have come to accept.

***

My daughter did not die. I did not lose her in that way. I am lucky for my relationship with her and with my grandchildren. This does not negate that I also lost my daughter. This paradox took me a long time to acknowledge. I work now to relax and listen to the universe and accept its gifts. In my head, I know it's okay to seek joy; the shoes won't start dropping left and right. The evil won't sniff out happiness just to crush it. Laughter does not conjure violence. I am not that powerful.

The work I still have left to do, though, is to grieve for the mother I also did not have and to allow myself to grieve for the mother I might have been.

I will not bring down the heavens if I let tears fall.

Eat My Story

She only blesses my little heart
when it fills with slick, white capsules,
like the ones Alice took
to make her small or tall again.
She flies on the wings of prayer
under black skies
around hair pin curves
sliding on ice. *Eat my story*
my mother says. *Swallow it whole. Don't forget*
the version. Don't forget the truth
within my pages. It's more vital
than Latin Vulgate; it's what glues
the family together. *Bless your little heart*
mother says
only when I am sick
from Chicken Pox, Pox
on my body, Pox
in my throat, struck numb, she makes me
eat her story, again and again
until I can swallow without choking,
spit it out whole.

Poetry Saves My Life

Floating from restaurant work to dancing in bars late nights to lazy mornings, I vacillate from near-alcoholic to college graduate to suicidal to dedicated mother. One morning, as my girlfriend and I lounge on a futon mattress with her two cats, the phone rings. The Director of the Creative Writing program offers me a Teaching Assistantship in an MFA program in Richmond, Virginia, a school within easy weekend driving range of my daughter. *Thank the goddess for a wisp of hope.*

I half joke that I scratched words even in the womb, but I scribbled on paper before I could form real letters, then moved into various obsessed states of writing. Most recently, in the past few years, no longer trusting in the privacy of journals, I would wake in the middle of the night with paper and pen to scratch out poetry about melted candles, single tears, loss, the abyss of death. I enrolled in poetry classes that kept me sane and I learned to focus on specifics to gain the universal, to focus on craft rather than just vomiting emotions on a page. My professor encouraged me to apply for the MFA and now my work has paid off.

Everyone thinks my inner free spirit is guiding me to the land of fairies and hippies after I switch from a psych degree to an MFA in poetry, but these become the most real, connected, authentic years of my life—in living as well as in writing. No one allows you to shun truths here; you cannot lie in poetry. Our writing group pushes each other to extend our metaphors, to use Eliot's objective correlative. To consider vehicle and message. No word wasted. No word accidental.

I am ecstatic to work with Dave Smith, a man I respect unabashedly. In his workshops, you learn that to succeed, you must put poetry above all else. Compare yourself to Yeats and Plath, not to each other. Push poetic boundaries. Find an aesthetic with a purpose, then hang your words on it. Later, I learn which truths to apply and which to question.

During the MFA, I live on $7500 a year, just enough to pay the rent and keep the lights on and the water flowing, usually. Occasionally I toss the *I-Ching* to decide between cutting off the phone or the lights, and I survive mainly on angel hair noodles and cigarettes, but when I live by candlelight, I cannot type my papers. Bogart's back-room expects our poetry crew each Wednesday night after work-shops. Greg Donovan, poet, joins us on many of those nights as we argue about, praise, or recite poetry and imagine ourselves aesthetic activists like the Agrarians or the Moderns. *Look at us, forging a new landscape, making the world a better place through writing: the world will know us!*

Sometimes we end up in someone's living room or on someone's porch, Greg pulls out the harmonica or guitar, all of us singing Indigo Girls, Janis Joplin, something painful and bluesy and, against all odds, hopeful. We cover each other in purple crepe paper and dance our way home. Other nights we skinny dip in the James, tell ghost stories and grab coffees and milkshakes at Aunt Sarah's Pancake house when it's still 24 hours, occasionally forgetting to wash the dirt of the river or body paints off our faces. Our group does not reach pinnacles of fame, but most of us become authors, teachers, philosophers.

As Teaching Assistants, we learn how to conduct ourselves in the classroom, but we also seek genuine connections, so at times we reveal more about our lives than we're ready to reveal. We smoke cigarettes and chat with our students in the Commons for hours. We take risks that sometimes go badly awry (such as one teacher who wants to bond with her students by emptying out her purse as an exercise in semiotics, but she hasn't gone through her purse in advance...think condoms, a pair of underwear, a resin-laced pipe) and sometimes works wonders (sitting on the floor with students; sharing pertinent personal stories; sharing some of our writing). We remain good teachers because we remain wide open, but now we understand the importance of boundaries. I still find folders of student thank you cards, evaluations, and even one blue book filled with expressions of gratitude for my ability to listen and make them feel safe.

Even through the pain of not raising my daughter full-time (each weekend, a friend and I carpool to N.C. to be with our children), this is the happiest time of my life—rife with connection and language and lessons in need of learning.

Blind Leading the Blind

I hook up with several artists in my 20s and 30s. During sex, I ask them to draw me dead. No one finds this intense or exciting or sexy. No one paints me dead. I move to the next artist; *please, paint me dead*. This is a pulsion toward both life and death.

One evening I seduce a lover into feigning blindness with me; we memorize each other's bodies with our hands. A greedy inventory catalogs her long curved lashes, rounded cheekbone, stark chin, slope of the neck leading to the most perfect breasts, a small mole on the left. The body dips and curves, her arm crooked from leaping out of a window when her brother said they could fly. Pixie Stix failed to work like Tinkerbell's fairy dust and her brother did not leap after her. Her hip slightly off center from a car accident. One knee turns in and the other slightly out. She's crooked and beautiful and broken. She whispers, "I'm so fucking in love with you."

We recite poetry, both the famous and our own; read *Lord of the Rings* aloud to each other and begin imagining wraiths in the real world; we march for gay rights and women's equality. We walk the D.C. Mall with the entire AIDS quilt laid out and we carry signs reading "Pussy

Power" and "Gay Rights are not Special Rights." We play bongos and leave our shirts in our backpacks. Who could deny us anything? Life has to be on an upswing, right? Justice will prevail.

Years later, I will break up with her in the bath. The night before, I found her, once again, drunkenly making out with another woman. She will say, "You are beautiful" and I will say, "I am not happy." She will burn down the Christmas tree. Even now, decades later, I can feel her on my fingertips. I could taste her out of a line up, identify her double helix core.

Spin Cycle

I sprawl in warm laundry on the floor. I am not a child. I am in grad school and I am crazy. My roommate tells me that she wishes she could reach out a hand and bring me to the other side, but it's not possible. She says she knows how I feel, there, on the hardwood floor, covered in random items of clothing, stuck, but that *she* rose up and found cycling and lovers and joy and purpose. She promises I will rise; she says to hope, but hope is not cake we can slice and share. Hope is insular and selfish and consumable only for those who hold it. When you let it go, it becomes vaporous.

When the laundry cools, I am lying on someone else's underwear. Someone else's cold underwear. Perhaps depression works this way—sit in the fire of doubt and hyperbolic pain until it grows cold and alien, until you cannot bear this exaggerated reality any longer and rise.

Insomnia

4 a.m. again. Waiting for the sun to rise so sleep feels safe again.

My windows rolled down, the slight promise of dew lingers. I am cruising. The houses and apartments remain dark for the most part; everyone living their Audenesque, doggy lives. A few random cars pass.

My cassette tapes have cycled through the Eagles' "Desperado" and "Southern Bridges Road." The rock station played Skynyrd and AC/DC, then I slid back into cassettes with Cocteau Twins and Dead Can Dance and now I am onto Laurie Anderson. *Oh boy. Right again.* Does Laurie Anderson know that people drive around listening to "Superman" and "X=X" when they have insomnia? Probably. *P.S. I—I feel—Feel like—I am—In a burning building*

When I need to ground myself from depression or anxiety or drugs and I can't drive, I write crazy small. Microscopically small. You can read it only if you have eagle eyes like I do. Then, I fold open my dictionary to a random word that serves as my answer to whether I should live or die that day. All entries in the *OED* point to LIVE. *Osmosis. Overcome. Ovulate.* I rest my head on the page.

Facts

- Hardly anyone pronounces sloth correctly; it rhymes with "slow."

- When you die from CO_2 poisoning, your skin turns black.

- If Catholics believe in transubstantiation, they are, indeed, cannibals.

- No one pronounces forte correctly; if you want to be strong in a talent, this should sound like an army fort. If you want to sing loudly, you would use for-TAY.

- The Witching Hour is 3:00 a.m., not midnight.

- The color you see in perfect darkness, is "eigengrau," or intrinsic grey.

- The MFA is a terminal degree, but you can't make a living off it.

Georgia: Seeking the Doctorate

My white cotton nightgown blows slightly against the wall, fluttering against the heating vent; its persistence mesmerizes me. From the bathroom floor, I know the bath is full, just the right temperature, but I cannot make it to the water. Unknown to me, my girlfriend of five years sprawls on the other side of the door, as she has done for many years, not wanting to invade my privacy, listening for sounds of dying, the stillness of suicide, perhaps even hoping on a teeny, unutterable chance that her vigil might finally cease. It's years after Sofie ends the relationship that I learn she finally could not bear the waiting, the waiting for me to live or die. We knew that if love could cure me, I would be hale and healthy, but daily high-priority panic breeds apathy. My well-honed survival mechanisms turned to self-defeating protections.

The night I fell in love with her from a simple touch, a hand to the small of my back in an evening of despair, I was house sitting for a friend. New Year's Eve, I counted out the dog's Valium, the acet-aminophen and ibuprofen, and purchased the Southern Comfort; no one would notice me gone for at least 24 hours, but then Sofie and I met on a happenstance. Stopping by a friend's on a final errand, I fell for her when she placed her palm on the small of my back and asked if I wanted more coffee; a simple tenderness that broke me, one small pat that I couldn't recall feeling from any other human being, not even my parents. She had been released from rehab a few months earlier, and I was not wedded to drinking or using. She loved discussing books and the arts and the complexities of life. Throughout our relationship we'd talk cosmography and Gericault and T.S. Eliot and Kristeva. We'd talk *Star Wars* and *The Pinball Wizard*. We talked sobriety and excess passion. She was financially stable, intense, artistic, and solid.

On our first real date, we both saw ethereal silver threads linking our souls in the ethosphere. We read *Jonathan Livingston Seagull* and all that Richard Bach proclaimed about soul mates and dream traveling. We promised to meet on the *Sea of Tranquility* at midnight; no matter how cold or dark the world turned, our love would sustain us.

We riffed through feminist theories, 12 Step Recovery, rules of engagement, and couple's counselors. We knew betrayal and honesty, boundary crossing and empowerment, but we played house like everyone else, imagining our 3BR/1B house with its large front porch, swing, a fenced-in backyard, and the perfect kitchen would make us okay, grown up. Would make us home. It almost worked.

Both of us suffering from as yet undiagnosed clinical depression, in hot, sticky, Georgia summers, sometimes only the fact that we left our cigarettes in the living room would drag us out of bed and into the day. We beat the new *Star Wars* game in 11 hours. I played until the sand people overwhelmed me and she'd come to my rescue before returning to sketching, drawing, or crafting jewelry. She was a fixer; so I added on broken moments to gain her attention. When she delved into her art, I wrote poetry, plodding and uninspired, or rollicking but sentimental. Words escaped me when I tried to shape them into metaphor or meaning, so I penned letters trying to connect with old friends. I checked the return mail every day, but folks rarely wrote back. I stopped checking the mail.

We were ridiculous, but not for the reasons we thought. She promised to help me get my daughter back when we *truly settled down*. We hugged and held hands in public and she taught me to take myself more seriously, but when we fought more than played, and I worried that she didn't want me because I wore a size 12, I began making dinner loaded with secret lard. She was vegetarian. I fattened her up and hoped she would stay. She gained weight and wondered what in the hell was wrong with her metabolism.

Her leaving wasn't about my size 12 body, of course; she found a 300 pound woman, one of our closest friends, to begin her transition away from me. We tried to make up once, on Valentine's Day. At the local furniture store, in a grand, desperate gesture, she bought a love seat for me and a chair and ottoman for herself. Oversized and awkward, this love seat's burgundy and green striped color scheme never matched anything else I owned, but I kept it for twenty-five years, even after it sagged in the middle and cats had nearly shredded the arms to the bone.

When we finally ended the relationship for good, I spent a summer homeless in Atlanta, living out of my car, hopping on a few friends' couches here and there, and visiting for long weekends with my daughter. My parents never knew; what would homelessness do to an imaginary custody agreement? I was able, now, to take Nicole to movies and the park and to McDonalds.

Somehow I passed Medieval Lit, the only doctoral course for the summer. Mostly, I kept plugging along.

The Edge of Entropy

Hot, dog days of Atlanta, no girlfriend, no 3-BR home, no bathroom of my own; my car my only constant; occasional friend's couches and extended visits to N.C. save me. It's that time of day where I consciously decide to test the higher power again. Today, I choose the little 5-points intersection; it's fairly early. A few store owners smoke at their door fronts, some young people are still out from their nightly adventures, one man plays bongos and a small crowd gathers. Patchouli and cigarette smoke hang heavy. No one will notice me. I move toward the larger intersection, away from shops, close my eyes, hold my arms wide, begin to make my way across the lanes slowly.

I am still testing the 7-year-old's theory that I will live to 35; I am not there yet. I am reaching for lightning again. I am calling for the Higher Power; if something higher than me exists and wants me to live, I will make it across.

I make it across.

I keep testing. I sleep with doors unlocked. Sleep with risky people; I mix uppers and downers and drive fast and close my eyes around danger. I snort eight balls and chase lines with Xanax and vodka mixed with bright blue Kool-Aid. Each weekend after I leave my daughter, I rebel against myself in the worst ways; once I head to the corner billiards bar in Decatur and find the loneliest looking man I can find. I buy him many drinks. We don't talk much, but he seems flattered, or honored, or desperate. The bartender keeps trying to catch my eye and twirls a finger around his temple, but crazy never dissuades me. I seek it on nights like these.

When we both can barely stand, I drive us to his home. He lives in one bare room, a greyish mat and a flat, striped pillow on the floor. One brown, plain box sits to the side where he says he stores his war stuff. A vet. I just wanted to forget my own battles and losses, but in the middle of sex, he cries, asks to stop, and, *oh shit,* maybe I have betrayed both of us by pretending that sex can be always just body, by pretending I didn't know that he wanted more than just fucking, but I feel nothing at this moment; I don't want to know his name or his story; I don't want to listen to his need for connection; I don't want to console or comfort. I want only escape from the chaos I do not want to feel, so I leave, drunk, stumbling, lost to this place and face of a scraggly vet who is still crying, naked, on a flat mattress, now even more alone.

I had taken him because of his weakness. I was the predator.

I have no tools with which to fix this.

Tar Baby

In the backseat of my car, the Tar Baby from the *Uncle Remus* stories sits calmly, just sitting. Anger engulfs me, oh, I see how Brer Rabbit must have felt, how he wanted to punch this irritating and smug figure, how he sits and smirks and refuses to respond, so I punch as hard as I can with my right fist, but then it sticks, trapped, just like in the stories my grandmother read to me so long ago. I cannot believe this is happening to me, though, this cannot be real, so I move to put my feet against this figure, to pry my hand from the darkness, from this shadowy baby, but they also stick, sink, begin melting into ethereal tar. No one escapes the Tar Baby—if you fight, he holds on tighter. If you relax, you stare into the spiraled eyes of death.

I am dreaming.

Abuse is like the Tar Baby. You think you are free, then you find yourself frozen and trapped; depression is right hand sinking, fear of dentists left hand sinking, intimacy phobia left leg, suicide-is-the-answer right leg sinking, until finally you are chest-to-chest with shadow and only one of you can survive—the shadow self or the solid.

Sometimes, in the non-dream world, I still glimpse this entity in my rear view mirror.

I seek out a Jungian therapist.

Hot-lanta

In my doctoral program, I don't find a community like the one in my MFA program, but I find a blend of scholars, servers, drug addicts, activists, musicians, and more. Café Diem proves the focal point for building lasting friendships, fleeting but passionate crushes, and many castles in the air. European in its closeness and in its service, no one hurries in Café Diem.

Packed tight, cappuccinos and espressos flowing, Rick orders goat cheese and sandwiches on baguettes, dark red wines and pastries; he and Heather order in French. I learn the hard way that IBS and café au laits do not mix, but I want to connect over bowls of rich coffee and steamed milk anyway. Our rag-tag group believes we will foment rebellion, that we alone perceive the core truths in the universe— the economic inequalities, the racism, the homophobia, the sexism. We think change is brewing; this is the 1990s, for fuck's sake. Equality must exist right around the corner. Bill Clinton, in the early years, brings some hope.

We're a blend of heroin addicts and prostitutes, the abused and the abusers. We're a melting pot of HIV+ and refugees and upper-class and lower-class and middle-class. We have danced in the light of the moon, skinny-dipped in dangerous waters, painted our faces with menstrual blood. We dance on cars and in bars and on the backs of sofas and on table tops. We cry together and puke together and live together. We pop culture riff and sling faux insults that only occasionally go awry with sensitive souls who remind us to love more gently at times, that life doesn't always have to be a shitstorm.

We were wild then, and up in arms about many, many issues, but we remained optimistic for the most part. We survived, and ended up with smaller lives than we had imagined. Smaller, but good lives.

When They Tell Me That Taking Medication is a Sign of Weakness

To try and stay alive, I make a list of favorites—the smoky smell of sulfur on a match; the earthy and mineral smell of spring, bittersweet like Eliot's memory and desire; English Breakfast tea with milk and hot baths, cocoa without marshmallows, and vanilla bean ice cream.

This is not working.

I look over my list of people I am supposed to call when I feel this way—Jan for deep discussion or just to gossip; Michael for distraction; Sawyer for whatever intellectual or spiritual kick he's on about that day; counselors for true desperation or even hospitalization. My fingers will not dial; my mouth refuses to open.

I continue my letter project.

Periodically, I compose a suicide letter to someone who made an impact on my life. I don't reveal this usually, but occasionally when drunk, I let it slip. Friends become furious at this secret plotting, but invariably ask if I've penned a letter to them. Even if I have written a letter and filed it neatly away already, I always tell them,

"No, I have not written yours. How could I possibly say goodbye to *you?*"

Years later, when I have composed 25 letters, I lose them all in a move. I had filed them alphabetically in a wooden box I got from my poetry mentor, Dave Smith. The ship on the outside reminded me of *Moby Dick,* a tome that terrified me on a visceral level—the evil whale, the vile Ahab, the sperm scene of chapter ninety four—men bonding with men and destroying nature. Did some random thrift store shopper read my missives or did they just get unceremoniously chucked in the trash? I am pretty sure that the letter writing kept me alive for many years; if I fooled myself into thinking that I needed to say a personal goodbye to everyone I knew, then I would have to keep writing note after note just to stay alive.

I stopped writing letters, but I also read that most suicides leave nothing behind.

Red Flag

When you jump in the deep end and cannot swim, you try all sorts of incorrect maneuvers. You flail. You thrash. But the moment of no return occurs when you calmly begin pumping your arms up and down to the side, an autonomic response that fails to keep you afloat, when you cannot call for help or even speak. When no untrained person would recognize the danger. When even if they throw you a life preserver, you cannot reach for it, your arms locked up and down. Silently dying. That's where the truth lies. Body says, *pump your arms, don't scream, save your breath, sink.* This is what suicide feels like.

One-Night-Stand Failures

At the Metro, after she asks to do a line of coke off my leather jacket in the bathroom, Shelagh the exotic dancer agrees to come home with me, laughs and says she'll meet her "lesbian quota," then, at my house she just wants to dance and reveals her joy at not being objectified as I totally objectify her; then, the woman who sees my stretch marks and begins weeping about her dead mother, reveals that she is only 18, not 21, and asks if I will just hold her.

Don't people get the rules of engagement in one-night-stands? It's *all about* objectivity. No flashbacks. No grieving. No cuddling for fuck's sake. Just body, body, body.

Don't think of the daughter your parents stole from you. Or the virginity you don't remember losing or the times your father came into your room because you squeaked the bed. Don't remember putting deodorant on your fingers to cover the scent of you. Don't remember being a bad patient at an abortion clinic. Don't remember the sea of belt buckles. Just do body, no talking, and glorious sex without guilt, without love, without phone numbers or even last names.

In the world of one-night-stands gone wrong, I begin to choose men because society *says* they just want sex without emotion, but these men also reveal abuses and pain and some of them even cry. And once, right in the middle, one guy asks, "Are you ok?"

"Are you ok?" definitely violates every rule, shatters the paradigm, sends me scrambling for clothes and car keys, running away from anything that might make me tackle the chaos.

Chaos

Chaos was waking up with a crack whore and hoping she'd stay for breakfast.

Chaos was telling everyone to get the fuck out of my house because they smoked pot around my daughter when she visited, was my living room filled with drag queens when my roommate thought I was spending the night out, was my summer of homelessness that no one knew about except one friend who was jealous of the As I earned in Medieval Lit.

Chaos was sex so loud I could pretend not to be having it.

***

Chaos is the mosaic inside my body as I freeze during a dentist appointment, a pelvic exam, or when someone says, "I love you."

At 35,
I Thought I Would Die,
but I Lived

I sense the 7-year-old me in the lightning storm and wish she could fly straight to heaven like Galahad, pure and perfect.

III
Crone

Adulting: Turning Points

At 36, a woman broke my heart for the last time.

At 36, Atlanta vanquished me.

At 36, Richmond called me back to pursue the writing life.

At 36, meaningful employment arose in the most unlikely of places.

At 36, I became a grandmother.

Grandma Cindy

Nothing prepares you for the unfettered love of grandparenting. You quit smoking. You consider buying a pearl-handled pistol in case someone even *threatens* to harm your grandchildren. You rock a child to sleep and remain stone still while she dreams on your chest for three hours. You love sleeping children; you can protect them and they feel protected; they love your newly squishy softness. As long as you are with them, nothing else matters.

Somehow, with grandchildren, you don't worry about fucking them up.

What to Tell Her

A counselor asks, "So, what guidance would you give your teen self to stop the suicide attempts, the cutting, the drugs, the indiscriminate sex? What would you tell her?"

I have nothing.

In this imaginary landscape with the power to help my former self without limitation, I have nothing. As a teen, desperate only for some sense of freedom to explore myself and the world around me, my parents scoffed, "You can't just have FREEDOM! That's ridiculous!" Setting my sights on busting barriers, I stole bologna and Bunny Bread and cars, fucked boys and girls, trading partners if the sex was not quite right, drank beer and popped pills, and ended up dropping out of high school and leaving home the day after my 16th birthday. When I left, I bussed tables and lived with Wendy W., her mom, and her twin siblings. Living primarily on Marlboro Reds, speed, and hot fudge sundaes at Mayberry's all-night diner, I somehow felt this simulated freedom.

Wendy and I wore roach clips in our hair, long feathers dangling from leather straps, even though pot made me vomit. She said we looked *Indian*. In an attempt to freak me out, she swore that her house sat on an old burial ground and that ghosts and apparitions appeared regularly, but I didn't freak out easily and I thought I had protections. My grandmother had weaved a tale for years that Cherokee blood coursed throughout our line (a lie I only unearthed in grad school). As a child, I posed for hours beneath our Japanese Cherry Tree, or the weeping willow, my legs *criss cross applesauce*, a roaring hot wool blanket around my shoulders, and a bandana around my forehead with a feather sticking out. I practiced patience. I practiced *one with nature*, allowing honey bees and yellowjackets to walk my arms, tasting my skin with their feet. I even wore moccasins for a while and even though the memory of this appropriation and privilege shame me to the core as an adult, the practice of sitting still for hours did teach me a great deal about the natural world and about acceptance. But in thinking of how to help the teen, telling her to take feathers out of her hair, to say it's appropriation or to forget about a possible Cherokee bloodline, that her life was not really freedom, would not have helped.

In order to help the teen, I needed to help the child, but what to tell that child before she turned into the libidinal, Thanatos-driven pre-teen? The words that others declared clearly didn't work: God would not give her more than she could handle; she should tamp down her hormones; "every dog has its day;" her parents would protect her from harm; she should stop running, stop being a chicken.

I tell her now that she is strong enough to survive and that running also requires strength. I tell her that healthy tools for survival exist and we will find them together. I tell her that being called a chicken doesn't lock her into the dare of living OR the dare of dying. I tell her that in the far future she may find neither permanent home nor contentment, but she will guide others to those at times. I tell her that she can protect herself from harm one day, that it eventually feels like enough, like freedom.

I stuff her belly so full of lies that she will never hunger again.

The High School Dropout Returns to High School

When I started teaching at the arts school, I was 36, just moved back from Atlanta to Richmond, and didn't trust myself fully not to say inappropriate things or to act inappropriately mainly because of my bluntness in regard to drug- or sex-related themes in literature (or real life). I also clearly love a good four-letter word and wondered if what works in teaching college classes might not work in high school. Even though I have always possessed a strong governor/censor in official places—I could wield the vocals and countenance to skim through church services without cursing or making overt waves—I feared crossing the line, but my pedagogical and personal background (and my Bachelors degree in Psychology) worked perfectly for this blend of urban and rural kids in a school for the arts.

As far as I know, I managed not to offend anyone too badly in the beginning, but my world changed irrevocably. I learned how to connect with teenagers (they're human beings—shut up and listen to them), make lesson plans (annoying at times, but simple), and confront many adults whose opinions on issues such as dress codes (sexist) and LGBTQ issues (sorely outdated and filled with homophobia and bigotry) and pedagogy (did they really still use worksheets and multiple choice only tests?) clearly needed challenging. I figured I was an excellent first year high school teacher to take on those tasks (*oh, silly first-year teachers*).

Many nights I worked until 3 or 4 a.m. and woke at 5 a.m. or 6 a.m. to begin again. Six classes; chair of two departments; expanding a curriculum.

One student wrote in his journal that the seniors bet I would last a month "but I know you won't even read this." I showed *them*; not only did I read every word they wrote, I am still here 18 years later. They left me notes like, "You might want to check your cleavage," when I inadvertently left a button undone. They left notes saying, "You did good today," and "U the realist person I know," and "thx for the sex ed talk" and "I am gonna miss you like an aborted poem." They made smiley faces and LOLs and pictures of dancing muffins who spoke encouragement. My classroom walls overflowed like a proud mother's fridge with scribbles and drawings and hearts.

Teaching teens can be painful, but nowhere near as painful as being a teen. We often want to mold them into our definition of good citizens, but to relate to them we must show humanity. To help them become good citizens, we must *be* good citizens—understanding, open, forgiving. To relate to them, you have to let them know that you understand the sex drive without being creepy. You have to let them know you understand the suicide drive without letting them know you still feel it. You have to let them know that you are a teen at heart while very clearly remaining the adult in every single situation.

Things I Say to Students

"Well, just tell your mom that when the penguins at the zoo sneezed on you, it turned you gay." This became a rainbow drawing on the whiteboard of the Literary Arts foyer.

"Well, if you're going to have sex, at least have good (and safe) sex."

"Wait. Stop talking. Write that down RIGHT NOW!"

"No, a baby cannot just FALL out of your vagina." (Spoken more times and in more situations than one might imagine.)

"Every grain of sand has gone through the body of an earthworm." This statement is actually not true, but it got their attention and they never forgot carpe diem poetry. They still send me memes about worm copulation.

"Your story is important to me."

My students name me a mom-dad. I feed them protein bars and bananas, listen to their heartbreaks and rants, but when I am pissed, my students present me with a physical copy of the "Most Fire

Email" and the "Most Shady" award. One student says I need to sit down with every kid in the school and give them life skills—stuff like: how to avoid getting pregnant; how to get pregnant; how to have safer sex. I should explain calmly that LGBTQ issues are not that complicated and that it's not really so hard to treat people equally and equitably and well—including yourself, especially yourself. I should look each student in the eye and say, "What happened to you was not your fault. You are still a child. That was not your fault."

At times, I still feel like a fake, a sham. We chat; we read; we chat; we write; we chat. But when they write about the time the boy next door touched them and they link it to an eating disorder and the metaphor is a morning glory and the writing is so lovely that my heart breaks open, I know that even if I am not a *real* high school teacher, I at least know how to create safety. Something I never really knew myself.

Sacred space. That's the alpha and omega of it all.

Façade

In the mornings, I don't fry that fresh farm egg, make wheat toast, steep the tea in one of my many tea pots or coffee in my French Press. The anxiety settles in my chest, in my brain, like a living shadow, creeps into my Eustachian tubes. I am living panic in a shell of calm. When my partner invites me to watch the meteor shower with him, I lie on the loveseat and watch him through the window wondering what the hell is wrong with me that I cannot join him outside.

Because I hold a full time job and am respected by my peers; because I inspire my students and have consolidated my debts; because I live in a lovely home and can joke about my mental health, my psychiatrist tells me I am no longer clinically depressed.

I want to kill myself to prove him wrong.

Barb

My counselor suggests that I name the ball of yuck that lives in my chest—name that feeling like when you're a drug addict and you can't quite reach the balance of your coke, Xanax, and hydrocodone, that feeling when you cannot get even one foot grounded and the vertigo sets in and you despair of ever feeling centered again. Those times when you cannot reason yourself out of the balled-up barbed wire binding your heart-chest-lungs. I name this ball Barb, and when Barb strikes, I say, "Okay gal, I am listening to what you want to tell me." Or at times I tell her, "Hey, I don't have time for this right now." I let her know we can chat later even if I'm lying.

My therapist initially wants me to call this ball of shame something minuscule, inconsequential, tiny like a piss ant, so I can squish her, but I am learning not to call parts of myself horrible names, trying not to kill myself in myriad ways, some creative, some mundane. So I allow Barb to nestle between my breasts and don't know if I can ever rip her out and send her to Antarctica or Greenland, but she is not pleasant, helpful, or romantic. She snarls, prickles, rages. Right in the middle of a lecture, she bangs against my heart, caging my breath, my memory. In the middle of writing or making love or playing with my grandkids, she whispers, "I could kill you right now."

Barb is me without my sense of humor, without support or strength, the deepest angst of a teenager rejected in first love, a cast-off freak; she lacks humanity, all shreds of self-acceptance. She is metastasized shame that may never heal.

Transmagnetic Cranial Stimulation (TMS)

A woodpecker taps incessantly at my left temple. On the large television, Niles and Fraser bicker as they find themselves desperate to extricate themselves from some scrape. Instead of killing myself, I try one last treatment. For two months, every Monday through Friday after work, my partner and I drive 50 miles each way to a small office where two former soldiers greet me, wipe off a dentist chair, strap me down, add a headset of sorts, and then calibrate a machine to my personal, unique settings. Transmagnetic Cranial Stimulation (TMS) involves no magnets, just a magnetic pulse that disrupts part of your brain (in a scientifically proven technique of course) and creates a "functional lesion" via a coil.

For 37 minutes a day I remain absolutely still, moving only my eyes and my toes, while an incessant tapping hits the left side of my head. In the beginning, I listen to music, try rock and roll, blues, gospel, but mainly I count the number of what they call pulses or taps. To me, it feels like a tap from a sledgehammer or a pulse from a small explosion, but I say nothing, just breathe and count. Eventually they turn on Netflix and I watch *Frasier* for the last few weeks of treatment. The antics of Niles and Frasier temper the excruciating pain.

I like the technicians, these former military men who suffered PTSD and recovered, and they chat with me or respect my silence, but they never ask how this feels, how painful I score it. Once, the lead psychiatrist bragged about their low rate of attrition and said they *had the process down* so it causes little to no pain. I wonder if they actually asked any patients. I never tell them that many depressed people fail to tell you when something hurts because that would imply hope for change. Plus, what's a little sledgehammer to the head each day? We probably deserve it.

But does TMS help? Yes. After about a week, I don't want to die every moment of every day. The world physically, literally brightens. My energy slowly returns. The litany of "You're fat and unworthy. You are a fraud. Kill yourself. Kill yourself," ceases cycling through my brain. I notice the dirt in my house and almost gather the energy to clean it. I want to make dinner and drag myself into the kitchen even if I never quite succeed in fixing a meal.

I don't suddenly leap up and begin dancing jigs or overcome my social phobias. I don't open up to the world in new ways, but I get out of bed, shower on most days, make a plan for work and stick to it. I gain follow-through and a bit of energy. I don't tell my colleagues, family, or friends. I don't want anyone to think that maybe I can want to live every day now, in my 40s, because if this works, does that mean that I held the power all along to want to live? Does this mean that I have to be okay forever?

I realize, though, that now I am simply in a place to deal with issues like the nondepressed do. You don't have to be depressed to feel love or lack or beauty. I understand John Gardner's Grendel, a monster torn apart by poetry.

What I Haven't Told You

I haven't told you that it set me free to admit to my daughter that I had been a bad mother. It released me from wanting to write an unwritable history. That I could just let the bombs drop and walk through unscathed. That she could yell or lie or manipulate me for money and I didn't have to care.

I haven't told you how well I lie.

Writers Retreat

At 49, for the first time since my MFA program, I focus solely on the art and craft of writing. Valley Haggard invites me on a women's writing retreat and in spite of my terror, I accept this triple dog dare, and it's the best decision I have made in years.

I am an adult; I choose self-care; I embrace good. I head to the mountains.

It's dark, either late night or early morning, and it doesn't even matter. It's the vernal equinox; a day for howling or dancing or watching fog rise over the creek. Books lining the shelves feel chosen just for me. The brass bed, the quilt-covered daybed, the high-back chairs—this Goldilocks loves them all; everything feels just right. The four other women and I meet to write, to eat, to write, to eat; Valley guides us through oceans of words and seas of stories and I may have died and gone to heaven.

In the group, I write:

The women in the house come and go, some loudly, some silently; the rooms tilt a bit like the Oz house on Beech mountain where my dad almost killed us in a hairpin curve, and my grandpa couldn't walk because the house gave him vertigo, and I said I felt dizzy and I stayed outside with him because the witch's shriveled feet sticking out from under the house signified danger to me. I don't think we were supposed to see or comment on the feet for some reason, but adults often reveal the most obvious dangers in ways that ring clear to children. Adults think they hide these signs well, profoundly. But I don't feel danger here, in this house, where women cry at stories you cannot cry about and now you feel them worth the telling and we accept each without question, and the women hug you even after you write that no one ever hugs you because you're so standoffish.

The women hug me again, all at once this time.

At the writers retreat, a parallax of women's lives and loves and loss humble me and embolden me and encourage me. They barrel through life with a bravery I rarely encounter these days—no shame, no blame.

When I leave, I determine to write the ruckus.

Thoughts to Take Away from the Retreat

1. People feel happier when you follow your dreams than when you hold back; martyr syndrome sucks for all involved parties.

2. My daughter is very, very angry.

3. My mother and my daughter are almost mirror images.

4. This home feels made out of my dreams. I even think I saw Keats in the garden.

5. Sometimes connections last and other times they won't, but the connection itself matters.

6. My partner sent me a picture of our cats sleeping on my side of the bed. This is a language of love.

7. After my father left, my mother read *The Five Languages of Love* and said that she had loved us all wrong. She didn't change a thing.

8. When we speak our shame, others help obliterate it.

9. Only I can tell my story.

Turn Your Shit Into Gold

Turn Your Shit into Gold is a prompt from Valley Haggard that sometimes inspires me and sometimes pisses me off. My stories feel more like polished turds lately, but I do own several polished dinosaur turds and they are quite beautiful. I also have some shit that is rough and raw and I don't see how it could ever tumble into some kind of sellable, smoothly packageable tale for the masses. One such moment is a time 17 years ago when I had moved back to Richmond after living in Atlanta. I decided to change the direction of my life, had accepted a position at a high school where I would teach talented young writers and make enough money to live on for the first time.

I decided to celebrate, headed for a beer at a local café where I had spent many pleasant hours over the years. I began chatting with a couple of clean-cut, pleasant men, probably in their late twenties; I was 36. We chatted about teaching—they said how much they admired teachers. One of their mothers was a teacher. They bought me a beer; I went to the restroom; when I returned, I took a sip from the draft and within minutes I was stumbling, blurry-eyed, apologizing for being so loopy, confused about feeling so drunk after only a few sips of a beer.

My memory skips and hops and rolls to the moment where we end up in a strange bed in a strange apartment and I am in the middle of sex with one of these men and I am not sure how I have gotten here and even though the memory is blurry and vague, the feeling of shame rings loud and clear. Oddly enough, what baffles me about this shame is not that I was ashamed that two men clearly roofied me on a night I was celebrating my new life. The shame is not from being drugged, nor from the physical violation. The shame comes because I had one moment of clarity where one of the men decided he couldn't do this and started to leave. The shame comes from me asking him to stay, from me, rising to my knees and literally begging him to stay; my shame comes from thinking he saw my stretch marks on my stomach and was repulsed; that he saw a body or a soul that was not worthy. My shame comes from thinking that once my entirety was revealed, I was no longer wanted.

I see this through a sheer memory of mosquito netting, a flash, a membrane between me and the rest of the world, I see this in the midst of what is a rape that I have called a roofie or night of unprotected sex or something else innocuous sounding. I see this through the sheen of another man who did not leave, who had no trouble having sex with a drugged woman. And I have done it again—I have said "having sex with a drugged woman" instead of rape. I am not sure why the shame settles into the place where I wanted the abuser to stay. I am not sure why the shame settles in the place where I felt unworthy. I am not sure why I have any shame at all. I am not sure why this shit rose and, I have to say, I sure as hell don't see the gold.

***

These days, as both a student and a teacher at *Life in 10 Minutes* in Richmond, I honor the magic of its process: in brief, you write in 10-minute (or eight-minute or twenty-minute) spurts and then read your piece aloud to others. I wrote the above piece in a 10-minute free write. After reading it aloud to the group, I confessed that I just felt shittier after writing it, that I wish I hadn't written it, that I felt yucky and hopeless and gross, but then, at the close of the session, a woman and writer I greatly admire came up to me, tears in her eyes, asked me for a hug, and said, "I have felt the exact same way. Not the exact same situation, but I have felt the rejection of the abuser and now I realize I am not alone." She said that hearing my words helped her make sense of the senseless emotion.

A year or so later, Tim M. asked me to read at a fundraiser for *Life in 10 Minutes*. I felt honored. When he mentioned that the theme was hope, I felt terrified. My writing does not often lend itself toward this theme. Then he replied, *sometimes the fact that we are standing here is enough to imply hope, sometimes the tentative "maybe" is enough.* I decided to share my story publicly because it illuminates the goal of writing and the really specific goal of the *Life in 10* mission. We write so that we do not feel alone. We read aloud so that others can respond in an immediate environment. We write messy and we emote messy and we can then revise or not revise, publish or not publish, do or not do, but we all have stories that need to be told for our own sakes and for the sake of others. Sometimes the goal is to tell something that feels horrible in the moment so that someone else finds a reason to carry on and that ultimately heals us as well.

After writing about that night and sharing it publicly, the shame began to lift. The details don't overwhelm me; the trauma is just a part of my past, not defining the way I move through the present, and isn't that the point of it all?

"So, how do you want to die?"

My counselor would never have asked this question a year ago, maybe not even six months ago. This query tests me, startles me, and pleases me. I know the ways I don't want to die—strangulation, suffocation, drowning, violence. But my first response is no longer, "by my choosing." I decide I want to die from "natural causes," my body shutting down from many years of use. She tells me to look forward. If I crave something unhealthy, I should ask, "Will this help me become more flexible, strong, long lived?" or "Will this help me die of natural causes?"

My choices are becoming easier.

Breaking Codependency

You realize that your nightmares about the *Uncle Remus* Tar Babies hiding in the back of your car may actually represent your mother because if she is no animal of love then what is she? She is like a stone-cold rock but a shadow of a stone-cold rock; you can't hug it; you can't punch it; you can't make it leave. You just stick to it like tar or like she is tar, gooey and rock-like but shadow Tar Baby.

The only sane path is to go it alone.

Write the Older Body

In my early 50s, at a wave pool at a theme park, the bodies fascinate me rather than depress me; what will they become, these jiggles and bounces and tightness; comb overs and braids; mimetic body stances? Fidgeting teens, teens who pump up breasts and suck in their barely-there stomachs, wear as close to thongs as the water park allows. Heavy women who reveal more than they intend as their bathing suits gap at the crotch. Skinny girls with nearly invisible cellulite waiting just underneath the skin to grow into maturity. Young men who carry themselves as if their lying-in-wait muscles have already erupted. They flaunt yearning in their bodies.

In my 40s, when I broke my ankle, I apologized to the EMT, "Sorry I'm so fat." He replied, "Well, you get more pain medication this way." Fat and Falling. Slipping off a curb, sliding on dew-covered clover, landing wrong on the ankle, feeling the *popping, cracking, breaking* to the right, and then *popping, cracking, breaking* to the left. *Every bone in my ankle shattered.* As my partner raced to get the car, I yelled at him to call 9-1-1 because I knew I couldn't lift myself into the car.

After my car accident several years earlier, I apologized to the EMTs as well. They laughed, then asked, "Are you diabetic?" *No. Just fat.* I wanted to go to the hospital because my vehicle had flipped a complete cartwheel after being T-boned by a huge SUV and I had blacked out for a moment, but I thought they might not be able to lift me onto the stretcher. I asked the EMT what would happen to my car and he said, "Someone will take care of everything." *At last, someone who would take care of everything.* Engaging in the ultimate game of trust, I fell backward onto their board. "I am sorry I am so fat. I am working on it—I just came from the gym." They smiled and asked again if I was diabetic. *I am not. I am just fat.*

Then at the beach I am 50 and I am fat and I am falling and I think, "This is why I fear the ocean. I have foreseen my death." A surprise wave wallops me; my knees shred, bloody on sand, too out of shape to rise on my own; other waves pummel me. My granddaughter has been knocked to shore beside me and I am trying to pretend that it's all okay, but I seek the lifeguard for the first time in my life and he's laughing at the people scrambling to rescue their water-soaked bags, towels, and flip flops and he does not notice me. A beached whale, I flounder; the mermaids do not speak to me. My granddaughter never seeks ocean water again.

Right now, my body and mind feel tired, rain weary. I bleed every 28 days, more regular than ever. I have perpetual PMS, migraines, irritability. I am not in menopause. The doctors don't ask about the last time I had sex anymore, they just say, "Hey don't be so fat," and I say, "Hey, I like my fat; don't take my body away; I worked hard for years to become sturdy and solid." In my thinnest years, I was a coke-head and a sex addict and a chain smoker and when people asked me my secret to being thin I said, "Try to kill yourself on a daily basis and you'll be a skeleton in no time."

Now, the pool presents a better option for me; sitting on the balcony allows me to enjoy the others leaping and frolicking in the surf. I embrace this body that carried me through childhood, and childbirth, and miles of walking and running and floundering and finding the right path again. It feels clichéd to say that these scars tell stories, but they do—the childhood bicycle crash blossoming on my knee, the stretch marks of pregnancy and childbirth, the car crash stitches-mark over the right eye, the slight white marks of cutting, the dot of an IV on my hand from the overdose, the broken ankle scars crisscrossing. Of course the outward scars are never the worst ones, but they remind us of what we survived. Whether we intended to or not.

So, What About Love?

A theme running through my circles lately: "Did anyone really love you?" or "Have you ever really experienced love?" I am not sure I understand mature, adult love. I ask two friends about this mysterious topic. I ask the first one why she loves her best friend, and she bursts into tears and says, "It has always been him!" because he could handle all of her personality. My other friend cries now because of the first friend who is crying and then she speaks of her new crush in terms of astrology and providence and dreams and all of the tears and the apparent wordless understanding mystifies me and I still don't know why we love some people and not others.

With all of my being I embrace love at first sight but not in the romance way—a kindred spirit love at first sight, yes, a friendship that mimics Homeric warrior bonds. Friends saved my life repeatedly.

I also believe love involves touch, the most basic of needs; babies die without it, but I want love quantified.

When my counselor asks me why I love my partner, I draw a complete blank. He cooks and cleans and fixes up the house and drives me at night when I can't see very well, but these do not seem to define love. When I picture him dead in our bed as I do most every night before I fall asleep, I do not feel happy. Once I have drifted off to sleep, he places my glasses carefully on the nightstand. It's an unspoken pact that he will care for me while I am sleeping, and this makes my imperfect life one of nearly perfect acceptance.

As I pull into my driveway, I see two small, light-up figures in front of the house—a blinking red nose, a white snarling, fuzzy Bumble. They're new to the yard, the only holiday decorations in the entire neighborhood. I thought my partner had not noticed my childlike wonder, my secret desire, when we ran across these objectively ridiculous *Rudolph* and *Abominable Snowman* characters at Big Lots, but here they stand, blinking and twinkling away. In a rush I have my answer—this is why. This is why I love him.

Perfection

Cycling through the daily routine of chastising myself for failing to be productive 24/7, I suddenly realize that I hold a vision of the world's population going through all the moments of their days in gleeful productivity: mastering challenging asanas in yoga and baking soufflés and running marathons and writing on a set schedule and meditating each morning and evening and when they get angry or upset—it's gloriously romantic and no one wastes an emotion. They create art out of every feeling and when they poop, flowers sprout, and when they make mistakes, they discover cures for cancer and their tears turn into diamonds and they are perfect all of the time while I sit and do nothing or maybe I watch a trivia or ghost hunter show on television and feel guilty the entire time and only more guilt comes from my emotions—no art. I don't stretch, much less do yoga, so one day I will have to buy a machine to put my socks on for me and in the mornings I limp down the stairs like my cat while I am sure others are waking like Disney princesses, or sprites through dust motes, except the perfect people don't have dust motes because the house is all sparkly and they take things *one day at a time* and they never light candles to cover up cat box odors, they only light candles when they make mad passionate love which is at least three times a week and they don't even plan date nights — sex just magically happens. Later they play with their children who never fight or rebel and everyone learns an important moral or ethical lesson each day and they end with hugs and conscious social and political action while I fall asleep after playing an electronic card game and being angry at my electronic partner, Bill, for not bidding the proper amount. Oh, Bill the electronic partner takes so much abuse.

That's all true, right? That is how the world works?

Sitting in It

I would rather sit in a mud puddle, a spilled drink, my own urine than to sit in my feelings. A huge fan of other people opening up, unzipping and spilling their stories onto the page, I admire them when they cry, when they laugh, when they are proud. I say, "I will bear witness to your stories," and I do. I say, "I will honor your stories." And I do. I cheer on the tears: "YES! Be awkward and uncomfortable! Challenge yourself! Write messy pieces that do not wrap up nicely!" I crave these stories.

All of that said, I hate to sit in my personal maelstroms. In the three weeks leading up to a reading about sexual assault, I could barely eat; I could barely function; I could barely stay in my shame-filled body. During the reading, however, a calmness and confidence settled over me. I needed to tell this exact story at this exact moment because someone needed to hear that they were not alone in that experience. The responses I received afterwards confirmed my gut instinct. The weeks that followed were a little raw. A little unsteady. But better.

One evening in class, I wrote that I could easily convince myself that the world would be better off without me. Quite logically.

That depression works this way. I then created an entire piece about how my will to live *always* takes over — positive and uplifting, I claimed that a little BoBo will-to-live doll pops right up and convinces me to stay in the world. Even as the words leaked from my pen, I knew I wrote them only because I sat in the "teacher's chair;" that saying *I want to die* would be much too shameful, and maybe too damaging, to reveal to students. On the drive home, I cried because the will to live does *not* always take over, that sometimes I am just too tired to die. This secret shame, when I keep it to myself, is the most dangerous of all.

I don't like to write about the various faces of shame — sexual abuse, intellectual elitism, depression, or implicit biases — because writing about shame and embarrassing moments feels terrible; however, I believe in the power of language to heal. I believe in the power of speaking our truths. By sharing, we become better people, we become more empathetic. This I have seen in action. I have seen the bonds that occur through sharing stories. Others often hold me up and I have helped to hold up others. We move forward through a balance of listening and sharing.

Shame originates from outside of ourselves, from society's warped messages and from leftover judgment that we internalized along the way. Shame whispers that we're better off dead or alone or silent; shame says that we are not okay. Each time I reveal another layer of myself and ask others to bear witness, the initial pain strikes, but the shame lessens, turns to smoke. The insecurity decreases. The friendships deepen. My will to live strengthens. I start to grab life by the tail again — this time for the right reasons.

Café Writing Day:
This is Life, Bitches!

I am a baby stealer. I see your baby's cherubic cheeks, red blossoms covering his pale face, blonde wisps flying crazy-like. I steal your baby and hold him up in the coffee shop like I am in *The Lion King* and I am screaming "This is life, bitches!" and no one notices me; no one sees me. This darling boy, haloed and staring without shame or worldly knowledge, gleams with simple enlightenment. I steal your gazes and I am bellowing, "Stop texting and Facebooking and FOMO-ing; look life in the face, bitches!" I say bitches because it makes me stronger in my imagination even though I never use the word in the real world.

So, why are you not falling on your knees in front of LIFE, in front of beginnings, in front of a lack of -isms, just blue-eyed openness without political thought of any kind? Schema and schemata forming images, mosaics in the brain and the baby incorporates me now, and he is not crying or clinging to grandpa or grandma, he looks me dead in the eye and assimilates me as I hold him over my head and roar, "I mean it! This is life, bitches! Dare to look. Dare to love it."

He doesn't blink.

I am a baby stealer. I steal the baby to stay alive. To keep my soul from shredding into tiny ticker tape pieces. I want to surround myself with babies, just watch them be alive — like those days I assign game days to my high school students so they can just be kids again, laughing with abandon, sitting on the floor or hopping on desks, just children and not small adults forced into worry and responsibility and heartache.

Those days when we're all just at play; all of us wild and innocent.

Wild Woman: What Wild Was

In the 4th grade, when a small group of boys mercilessly played keep-away with a kindergartner's shoe, I charged the whole group with a bellowing,"Give it back!" and they ran away screaming, "She's a wild woman!"

Wild was grass stains and polluted creek beds and neighborhood boys and crabapple fights and cigarettes and sex and whiskey and hitchhiking across the states.

Wild was climbing the Brooklyn Bridge hoping Rick would not backslide into heroin; wild was hanging on when everything inside of me said to let go and letting go when everything inside of me said to hang on. Wild was loving her and believing for a year she'd leave her wife but of course she never did, at least not for me. Wild was 95 mph down highway 85 to Atlanta and back again to see my daughter each weekend, then every other weekend, then once a month as she grew older and older.

Wild was writing all my final papers in a hotel after a hurricane while accidentally tripping on acid.

Wild was dancing naked with my eyes closed but my arms outstretched.

These days, wild is having a glass of wine without taking an antacid; watching horror movies with my granddaughters; drinking coffee after 4 p.m.; publishing my memoir in pieces.

Wild is hope, man. Pure and simple. Hope without a landing pad.

Colophon

Wild Woman was typeset in Freight Text and Lydian.

Freight Text is a serif typeface designed by Joshua Darden and published through GarageFonts in 2005. Freight is an extremely versatile superfamily with many different versions available, making it suitable for a wide range of typographic challenges. It is the type family used by the National Museum of African American History and Culture in Washington D.C.

Lydian is a calligraphic, humanist sans-serif typeface designed by Warren Chappell and released through American Type Founders in 1938. It was famously used on the end credits for the television shows *The Lucy Show* and *Here's Lucy* in the 1960s and 1970s.

Wild Woman was designed by Llewellyn Hensley & Content–Aware Graphic Design—**content-aware.design.**

Thank you
for supporting *Unzipped*

Our project is made possible by readers like you. We are infinitely grateful to our patrons who make it possible for us to continue publishing urgent, brave, and true stories! To learn more about supporting us through our subscription program, our online litmag, classes, and workshops, visit **lifein10minutes.com/unzipped.** We would love to write, read, and (metaphorically) unzip with you.

Issue 2 (coming out in early 2021) will feature writing by Kristina Cotis Hamlett! Hamlett is a writer, speaker, blogger and Strongman competitor. She is a graduate of Shenandoah University with a degree in Psychology.

She is the author of the E-book journal "What I Love About You: A Guided Journal to Writing Your Proposal and Vows." Her work has been featured on *kimberlyelise.com, mitchell-productions.com, 30seconds.com, foreverbemoved.com, The Churchill Newsletter, Life in 10 Minutes* and *Liminalities*. She currently works in human services and facilitates writing classes at a non-profit organization. She can be found at **kristinahamlett.com.**

CPSIA information can be obtained
at www.ICGtesting.com
Printed in the USA
FSHW020048280121
77980FS

9 781949 246063